Four Keys to Staying Full of God

An Introduction to

Discover the Keys to
Staying Full of God

Andrew Wommack

Published in partnership between Andrew Wommack Ministries and Harrison House Publishers.

Woodland Park, CO 80863 – Shippensburg, PA 17257

ISBN: 978-1-59548-652-3 *Four Keys to Staying Full of God*

For Worldwide Distribution, Printed in the USA

1 2 3 4 5 6 / 26 25 24 23

Contents

Would you like to get more out of this teaching?

Scan the QR code to access this teaching in video or audio formats to help you dive even deeper as you study.

Accessing the teaching this way will help you get even more out of this booklet.

awmi.net/browse

Introduction

Do you feel like your relationship with God ebbs and flows? Have you ever felt like you've had a mountaintop experience with God one day, then totally empty the next? Would you like to see more consistency and growth in your spiritual life? If you answered yes to any of these questions, then this teaching will help you reach a new level in your walk with the Lord.

When the Lord drastically touched my life on March 23, 1968, I was caught up in the supernatural love of God for about four and a half months. But it wasn't the emotional experience that sustained me through all these years of life and ministry. I had to make an effort to stay full of God.

Through studying the Word of God, I've discovered four basic keys that have helped me stay full of God. And because I put these truths to work in my life, my relationship with Him has only grown since then. I can truthfully say that my walk with the Lord has only increased. I haven't lost the benefit of that encounter with the Lord in over fifty-five years. It has only gotten better.

Maybe the Lord touched your life once, but now you feel distant from Him. If that's the case, it wasn't God's fault. Once you realize what's necessary for you to consistently experience His presence, I believe you will begin to see a constant flow of His goodness in your life.

The vast majority of people come to church looking for a feeling. They sing songs about how desperate they are for God's presence, and if they don't feel goosebumps, they'll walk away saying things like, "God wasn't within a hundred miles of that place." That should not be the typical Christian experience.

The Lord wants you to be blessed more than you do. He wants to have a close intimate relationship with you—but He's not going to force Himself on you! If you feel far away from God, guess who moved? It wasn't God. He will never leave you or forsake you (Heb. 13:5). It's our hearts that become insensitive to God. His heart towards us never changes.

There are steps you can take to maintain the fullness of God in your life. And I believe if you follow the keys I'm going to share in this booklet, you'll experience Him more than ever before!

Made to Last

Years ago, I was ministering at a church in Louisville, Kentucky. On the morning before my final evening session, a woman came to me with tears in her eyes. She said, "This teaching has just transformed my life. I've never understood how much God loved me until this weekend."

That's awesome! But then she said, "I am just enjoying the love of God more than I ever have in my life, but I know it won't last." She thought it was like a feeling that would wear off after a month or even a week. It really grieved and bothered me to know that someone would expect God's love to just stop impacting their life.

I'm not condemning this woman, or you, if that is your experience. I acknowledge that's the way it is with most people, but it's not how it is supposed to be. As the hymn goes, "Every day with Jesus is sweeter than the day before. Every day with Jesus, He loves me more and more. It gets sweeter as the days go by." That should be the normal Christian experience.

So later that day, I went back to my hotel and spent all afternoon praying and thanking God that what He's done in my life has never diminished—it's only increased! To understand why it's been that way with me, you have to know a little of my background. I was raised in a church that taught people are like buckets with holes in them. You can have your bucket filled up, but it will eventually drain out. So, according to that way of thinking, you've got to be filled again and again—constantly having God touch your life again. I was taught that the Christian life is like a roller coaster with constant ups and downs. That's not true!

On the contrary, I'm thankful that God touched me, that I was filled with His love, and that I have never lost that fullness. God has explained so many things to me, and I have so much more understanding than I did then. Instead of losing the revelation that God gave me, it has only grown and increased. I really believe this is the way the Christian life should be. You go from glory to glory (2 Cor. 3:18), not from pit to pit.

Find the Keys

*For the invisible things of him from the creation of the world are clearly seen, being understood by the things that are made, even his eternal power and Godhead; so that they are without excuse: because that, when they knew God, **they glorified** him **not*** *as God, **neither were thankful**; but became **vain in their imaginations**, and **their foolish heart was darkened**.*

Romans 1:20–21

There are four keys in verse 21 (above) that describe the steps you can take both to draw near to God or walk away from Him. For example, maybe the joy of the Lord is not as strong in you today as it once was in your life. If you've ever known God's love, but you aren't experiencing it today as you once did, there were steps you took away from Him. You may not have walked away intentionally, but you that stopped the flow of God's love. It wasn't the Lord that decreased His love in your life. However, if you repent, you can use the same steps to come back to Him.

If you've ever traveled, you'll know what I'm talking about. If someone wanted to know how to get from our Charis Bible College here in Woodland Park, Colorado, to Denver, I could tell them where to turn and how many stoplights they'd have to go through before they got out of town. I could also tell them where to turn to reach a major highway and head toward Denver. If they wanted to turn around and head back to Charis, I could use the same directions but apply them in the opposite direction.

The apostle Paul gave us a spiritual roadmap in Romans 1. Verse 21 tells how people distance themselves from God, and the following verses (vv. 22–28) reveal milestones on the way to becoming reprobate ("rejected by God and without hope of salvation").[1] In the same way, we can apply those four keys in a different way to stay full of God and turn away from a dangerous path, which includes rebellion, idolatry, and sexual sin (including homosexuality).

Expressed negatively, as in this verse, the four keys are:

1. They glorified Him not as God
2. Neither were thankful
3. Became vain in their imaginations
4. Their foolish heart was darkened

These same four keys expressed positively are:

1. Glorify God
2. Be thankful
3. Recognize the power of your imagination
4. Have a good heart

Depending on how you walk out these four progressive steps in your everyday life, you are the one who determines whether or not you stay full of God.

Glorify God

The first key to staying full of God is to glorify Him. The word *glorify* means "to render (or esteem) glorious."[2] To *esteem* something means, "to set a high value on" or "regard highly and prize accordingly."[3] In other words, if you quit valuing or prizing what the Lord has done in your life, you won't stay full of God. In contrast, you can actually increase the value of what God has done by glorifying Him.

Glorifying God has been a major aspect of my life. When the Lord really touched my life as a teenager, I'd already been born again for ten years. But that night, I had an encounter with God, and He just showed me what a total religious hypocrite I was. I may have been born again, but I was trusting in my own goodness. I was trying to earn God's favor by doing good things. So, I was making myself my own savior instead of approaching God through Jesus as my Savior.

After the Lord revealed all of this to me, I repented. I expected rejection and punishment. But instead, a tangible love of God just flowed over me. And I was overtaken by the glory of God. My awareness of God's love and His presence with me transformed my life.

I began to place so much value on what God did in my life that nothing else could compete with it. In Luke 14:26, Jesus said,

> *If any* man *come to me, and hate not his father, and mother, and wife, and children, and brethren, and sisters, yea, and his own life also, he cannot be my disciple.*

In Matthew 10:37, Jesus taught something similar—simply stating that we should prefer Him above any other relationship; but in Luke, He said that to be His disciple, you have to love God more than you love your father, mother, brother, sister, or even your own life. Now, Jesus isn't saying that you're supposed to actually hate yourself. But you should value and prize God greater than your own life or any other relationship. The verse is talking about relative worth and value.

I've never been the same since the night the Lord "rang my bell." As of this writing, that's been over fifty-five years ago; and I can truthfully say that the encounter I had with the Lord that night when I was eighteen years old is more real to me today than it has ever been.

Value God More

Let's say the Lord touches your life and reveals His unconditional love toward you. You receive the peace, joy, and other benefits that revelation brings, but tomorrow the devil will agitate someone at work to come over and dump on you. They'll criticize your performance or something else the devil knows will bother you.

Do you know what's happening? The enemy is competing for the value you placed on God and His love. He is trying to get your eyes off Jesus and looking at others criticism of you. You can go to church on Sunday morning and get so blessed and happy. Then, by Monday morning, someone has jumped all over your case. Satan is trying to steal your joy. But if Satan can't get you to devalue what God has done in your life, then he can't steal God's blessings from you.

It's like riding a seesaw: one end is the value you place on what the Lord has done in your life, and the opposite end is the value you place on things or what others say.

What the Lord has done in your life

The value you place on things

When one side is up, the other side is down—and vice versa. If you value what God says, you just have to devalue what others say.

Years ago, in one of the churches I pastored, I gave a sermon on not being someone else's trash can—not letting gossip or criticism get inside you. It had such an impact that when one of our church members later heard someone being critical, he put his hands on his head and acted like he was putting a lid over himself. He wasn't going to let someone else's negative opinion compete with God's Word!

God loves me, and I will not let anyone dispute that. Not only does He love me, He likes me. I like to say that God carries around a picture of me in His wallet! Amen! Now, I'm not being prideful. But I value my relationship with God more than I value my relationship with anyone else—even my wife! Some people may think, *Well, it shouldn't be that way. Your marriage or your family should come first.*

There is nothing that even comes close to God in my eyes. My wife knows I love the Lord far more than I love her. I also know that she loves Him much more than she loves me. Instead of this detracting from our relationship, it's a blessing.

When Jamie and I first got married, we struggled financially. Some people say they're broke when they have more bills than money. When I tell you that we were broke, I mean that we had nothing, zero, nada, zip! I would have to go out, pick up empty bottles, and return to a redemption center just to have enough money to put gas in our car. We would go two weeks at a time with no food when Jamie was eight months pregnant.

Once, during a flight, I watched this movie about a guy whose wife left him because of the financial problems that they were in. Considering what we went through during the early years of this ministry, Jamie could have left me. But do you know why she didn't? It wasn't because I'm such a great person. It was because she loves God more than me. She made a commitment to God *and* to me, and I take great comfort in that.

It's Your Choice

Not long after I got a revelation of God's glory and His love for me, I felt like He told me to drop out of college. This was during the Vietnam War, so for me to follow God in this way meant I could be immediately drafted and sent to Vietnam. I also stood to lose the Social Security income that I had been receiving since my father's death when I was twelve years old. I could keep this income only as long as I was still in school.

Following the Lord would cost me financially. I would also end up with a first-class ticket to a war zone where I quite possibly could have been killed. Beyond that, every person in my life who I ever respected told me one way or another, "This isn't God." Even leaders in my church told me I was hearing the devil.

It seemed like everyone was telling me what a dunce I was and how I shouldn't be going against the way things were always done. I wasn't trying to rebel against the advice of well-meaning people; I just wanted to be obedient to what I knew God was speaking to my heart.

Because of all these negative reactions to my desire to leave school, I backed off from following the Lord's leading for a while. During that time, I was absolutely miserable. This continued for two months until I couldn't take it anymore. Then one night, the Lord finally spoke to me through Romans 14:23, which says, *"Whatsoever is not of faith is sin."*

I realized I was in sin because of indecision. I determined to make a faith decision that night and stick with it. As I prayed and studied the Word for guidance, I found Colossians 3:15, which says, *"And let the peace of God rule in your hearts."*

The Lord spoke to me that I was to head in the direction that gave me the most peace. To be honest, I didn't have total peace in any direction, but just as an umpire has to make a decision and stick with it, I needed to make the call. I had the most peace about quitting school, so that's what I did. I stepped out of indecision and into faith, to the best of my understanding.

Within twenty-four hours, the Lord gave me such confirmation and joy that I have never doubted the wisdom of that decision since. I glorified God and did what He told me to do despite the criticism of nearly all my friends.

Immediately after that, the devil came to steal the word God spoke into my life. After I had a pre-induction physical for the army, which I passed, an army recruiter then came to my home to show me all the advantages of volunteering instead of being drafted. I go into more detail about this in *Discover the Keys to Staying Full of God*, but in a nutshell, this recruiter ridiculed the value I had placed on what the Lord spoke to me.

I was obeying the Lord and trusting Him for my future. I left the matter in the Lord's hands and didn't feel like I needed to volunteer for the draft. This recruiter laughed at my faith and told me, "Boy, you are going to Vietnam!" He didn't value the word of the Lord the way I did, and it made me mad. I punched him in the chest and told him that God was bigger than the U. S. Army or every demon in hell.

What I was doing was keeping my value on what the Lord spoke to me as greater than what an army recruiter had to say. Many people would have caved right there; and like that seesaw, as they increased the value on what a government representative said, the value they place on what God said would have decreased. I could have lost the benefit of my encounter with the Lord right then. But praise the Lord, I kept esteeming, valuing, and glorifying what the Lord spoke to me above all other voices; and my joy and benefit of that has not waned.

That one decision, possibly more than any other, set my life on a course that has brought me to where I am today. If I would have listened to all those other people, and not followed God, you may have never heard of me. I made it here only because I valued (glorified) the Lord over the opinion of everyone else in my life.

Make God Look Bigger

Another way of glorifying God is to magnify Him. This is really important. You can magnify things in your heart. You can make things appear bigger, including God. That same word translated *glorified* in Romans 1:21 is also translated *magnify* elsewhere in Scripture.[4]

Now, God is who He is regardless of what you or I think—we can't change who God really is. But as far as your experience with Him goes, it is completely up to you how big God is in your life. You can either make Him big, or you can make your problem big.

If the doctor says you've got cancer and you're going to die, you can start magnifying that. You can just fall apart like a two-dollar suitcase, or you can magnify the promises of God. You can say, "The first report is not the last report! I believe I'm going to see God's healing power manifest in my life, and this is going to work out for His glory!" You can use your mind like a pair of binoculars and either choose to magnify something or reduce it in your sight.

If you came to our Charis campus here in Colorado, you would see Pikes Peak right outside the window. Looking through a pair of binoculars would make Pikes Peak seem huge and closer than it is. You could see all kinds of details on the mountain. But you could take that exact same set of binoculars, turn them around, and you could shrink Pikes Peak so it looks tiny and far away. The same pair of binoculars can either magnify or decrease something, depending on how you use them. Your mind is like that.

Whatever you focus on gets bigger. If you focus on problems—like a bad report from your doctor or the amount of bills you have to pay—they will get bigger. Now, I'm not saying that you totally ignore problems. You need to confront things and deal with them head on, but you need to deal with them in the light of God's promises. You need to make what God has already done and who He is look bigger in your eyes than the problems you're facing.

One of our *Healing Journeys* testimonies is about a woman named Connie Weiskopf. She was given a cancer diagnosis, and her friends told her to learn everything she possibly could about cancer. But Connie had enough wisdom to say, "No, I don't need to learn everything about cancer I possibly can. I need to learn everything about healing that I possibly can."

That's when she found my materials and started learning about how God wanted her well. She came to one of my meetings, I prayed with her, and she was healed of cancer.

It was all because she chose to magnify the answer—God and His healing power—rather than the cancer!

Be Thankful and Not Anxious

Be careful for nothing; but in every thing by prayer and supplication with thanksgiving let your requests be made known unto God.

Philippians 4:6

The second key to staying full of God is to maintain a thankful attitude. The Greek word that was translated *careful* means, "to be anxious."[5] We aren't supposed to be anxious about anything.

Years ago, I was holding a series of meetings in Scotland. The H5N1 virus (also known as bird flu) had hit the United Kingdom with all its force and dominated the news. The authorities were killing birds by the thousands.

I watched a television interview of a leading medical expert in Britain who seemed like he was only trying to intensify the panic. When asked about the possibility of this disease mutating from birds to humans, he said it wasn't a matter of *if*, but *when*. Experts in Britain also predicted it would infect a significant portion of the world's population and kill many millions of people.[6] (This may sound familiar to anyone who remembers the doom-and-gloom predictions surrounding the 2020 COVID pandemic!) The H5N1 was in 2005, but at the time of this writing, there have been fewer than 500 human deaths attributed to the that strain of avian flu.[7]

The philosophy of the world is to overstate everything and predict the worst possible outcome. It's gotten to where the media doesn't just broadcast the nightly news; it's more like a nightly prophecy! But these spiritual forces are detrimental to our mental, emotional, and physical health, causing our world to become addicted to fear. If there aren't enough negative things going on to be anxious about, the media will create something for you.

I believe one of the greatest antidotes to worry and fear is thanksgiving and praise. When we thank God for all His blessings, it refocuses our attention to the positive things in our lives. Sure, all of us have problems. We live in a fallen world, but God is good, and God's goodness toward us is greater than all of Satan's attacks.

Every one of us has much to be thankful for and more than enough reason to praise Him. We just need to put everything into perspective. Paul praised God after being beaten, stoned, whipped, and thrown in jail. Then he said these were but light afflictions that last for a moment, and nothing to be compared to eternal things (2 Cor. 4:17–18).

Paul understood that praise coming from a thankful heart has great power. It will build you up spiritually, it is a source of strength, it is a powerful weapon against the devil, and it ministers to the Lord. Being thankful will help you stay full of God!

Don't Forget His Benefits

Bless the Lord, O my soul, and forget not all his benefits.

Psalm 103:2

The reason we are commanded to remember all of His benefits is because it is our tendency to forget. It takes effort and a choice of our will to remember, but it's well worth the effort. I often think back over the good things the Lord has done in my life, which keeps me full of Him and allows me to easily access all that God has for me.

If you're going to be thankful, it involves two things that are really important. One of them is memory. You can't be thankful for something if you don't remember what

God has done. The other thing is humility. When you say, "Thank you," you're acknowledging that somebody else did something for you.

Paul listed unthankfulness as one of the signs of the end times and put it in the same verse as covetousness, pride, blasphemy, and unholiness (2 Tim. 3:1–2). You probably wouldn't argue that we live in a society full of unthankful people, even in spite of the fact that we have more prosperity and opportunity than at any previous time of human existence.

Many people view thankfulness as optional, but the Lord listed unthankfulness along with other ungodly characteristics. It is a dominant characteristic of this age. Being thankful can be the difference between being healed and being whole (Luke 17:18). In Luke 6:35, Jesus compared being unthankful to being evil:

> *But love ye your enemies, and do good, and lend, hoping for nothing again; and your reward shall be great, and ye shall be the children of the Highest: for he is kind unto the unthankful and to the evil.*

Many people may say, "I'm a self-made man." But that's pride! Anyone who is wrapped up in themselves makes a pretty small package. But to stay full of God, you need to get to where you humble yourself and are constantly saying, "Thank you," especially to Him! You need to acknowledge the things that God has done.

For example, you may have worked forty hours this week and received a paycheck, but God is the one who gave you the health to work. He also gave you the talents and skills you use to earn a living. Maybe you've developed those skills and talents over the years, but God was the one who put them inside of you in the first place. So, even though you worked for that money, the Lord is the One who enabled you to do it, and you should thank Him.

There are many people who don't put in a full day's work for their employer—maybe they'll show up five minutes late, or they'll stretch their ten-minute break into twenty, etc. They act that way because they are unthankful. They don't value what God has given them.

Giving thanks is just a healthy practice. You can check your spiritual pulse by seeing how thankful you are. Whether or not you are praising the Lord and giving Him thanks is a tremendous indication of where you are in your spiritual life. It will indicate whether or not you are staying full of God.

Remember the Lord

Recounting what God has done has been super important in my own life. I can think of dozens of instances when the Lord saved my life. I bet God has also saved your life many times, but you have just forgotten. Now that I've jogged your memory, it may be coming back to you. If you would rehearse those victories and think about God's goodness, it wouldn't take long before any discouragement you are experiencing would just leave.

One time, a 2,000-pound, three-foot-tall boulder that was on my property rolled over my hand, arm, and head. This could have been deadly, but I immediately jumped up, started shouting the name of Jesus and screaming, "I'm healed! I'm healed!" About thirty seconds later, I checked myself, and everything worked the way it should. I erected a marker on that spot that reads, "August 25, 1999. Jesus saved my life when this rock rolled over my hand, arm, and head. Psalm 116:6." That verse says,

> *The Lord preserveth the simple: I was brought low, and he helped me.*

Now, that may be funny to you, but for many years after that, every time I walked past that spot on our property, I stopped and thanked God for what He had done.

Amen! I did a piece of stupid to cause that rock to roll over my head, but God preserved me anyway. Praise the Lord!

If you're depressed, you haven't been thinking about what God has done for you. Instead, you're thinking about what the devil is doing to you. You aren't focusing on the joy that is set before you. You aren't saying, "At the very least, if I die, I'll go to be with the Lord. If I'm poor, I have a mansion in heaven on streets of gold." You're just looking at your present situation and not evaluating it in the light of eternity.

You can't be depressed unless you've taken your eyes off Jesus and what He's done, forgetting His goodness in the past and forgetting the future He's promised you. You've just forgotten everything. If you want to be depressed, there are plenty of depressing things you can think on, but that only diminishes what God has done; and it won't keep you full of Him. If you look at things properly—being thankful and remembering God's goodness—you have no reason to be discouraged.

I often take time to recount the good things God has done for me, and that keeps me filled. I've seen my son and wife both raised from the dead. I've seen countless miracles in this ministry. I've seen the Lord provide for us numerous times. I've seen our Charis Bible College continue to grow and touch more lives around the world. There isn't a day that goes by that I don't think about what God has done and I stop to thank the Lord for His goodness.

As a matter of fact, if you come to Charis in Woodland Park and sit in our 3,200-seat auditorium, you'll see a scripture above the platform that expresses the attitude I try to maintain on a daily basis:

This is the Lord's doing; it is *marvellous in our eyes.*

Psalm 118:23

Adjust Your Focus

Enter into his gates with thanksgiving, and into his courts with praise: be thankful unto him, and bless his name.

Psalm 100:4

If you choose to always be thankful and glorify God, thanksgiving will force you to look beyond any negative report. It'll make you focus on what God is doing. Problems come to all of us, but what are you going to focus on?

If you went to the zoo and used a camera to take pictures, you can focus on an animal that's behind a chain-link fence and make the fence disappear in your sight as you adjust the lens. But you could also adjust the lens to focus on the fence and you wouldn't see the animals. It all depends what your focus is on.

One time, Charles Capps was telling God how things just didn't seem to be working out for him. The Lord stopped him and asked, "What are you doing?" Charles responded, "I'm praying." But the Lord corrected him by saying, "No, you're not. You're complaining!"[8]

Instead of entering *"into his gates with thanksgiving, and into his courts with praise,"* so many people come in and—in a sense—throw up on God. They come before the Lord and just talk about all of their problems.

Jesus taught us about thanksgiving in what's commonly called the Lord's Prayer (Matt. 6:9–15). He started by saying, *"Our Father which art in heaven, Hallowed be thy name"* (v. 9). When a person prays that, they are thanking Him that he's a Father, not just that he's God Almighty. There's intimacy there. You are thanking Him for that relationship. You're hallowing (honoring) His name.

Over the years, I've had a lot of women come to me seeking prayer for their husbands. Heartbroken, they would ask me, "What can I do?" And I tell these ladies that one of the first things they should do is quit praying for their husbands because what most people call prayer is just nothing but complaining. I've heard a lot of so-called prayers start out like this: "God, my husband's a reprobate. He beats me. He beats the kids. He beats the dog. He spends our money. He drinks all of the time," and so on. Then, after all that, they ask God to fix him! I'll tell you, finishing a prayer by saying, "In Jesus' name, amen" doesn't make it a prayer!

All they were doing was focusing on the negative and making the problem bigger. I'm not saying that problems don't exist, but you can say, "Father, I've got a problem, and you are so much greater than my problems." You could stand on a verse like 1 Corinthians 7:14 that says, *"For the unbelieving husband is sanctified by the wife, and the unbelieving wife is sanctified by the husband."* You can take God's promises and start magnifying Him instead of the problem.

If you would mix thanksgiving with your communion with God, it would magnify the answer instead of magnifying the problem.

See Things on the Inside

The third key to staying full of God is to use the power of your imagination. It is important to everything that God wants to do in your life. If you can't see things on the inside of yourself, you'll never see them on the outside.

For instance, people may pray for healing, but they've never seen themselves well; they see themselves sick. Vacations even have to be planned around allergy seasons, and medications are an important part of the preparations. Still, people's identity is sickness, and yet they're praying for health. It doesn't work that way.

> *Thou wilt keep* him *in perfect peace,* whose *mind* is *stayed* on thee: *because he trusteth in thee.*

> Isaiah 26:3

The word that was translated *mind* in this verse, is the Hebrew word, *yetser.* This scripture clearly links our peace to keeping our minds stayed on and trusting in God. This reveals that our emotions follow our thoughts. This is a major point that many psychologists miss. They say emotions are a result of circumstances. If that were so, then everyone who has experienced the same negative circumstances would have the same negative emotions. But that's not true.

This exact same Hebrew word is also translated *imagination* five different times in Scripture, including in Genesis 6:5:

And God saw that the wickedness of man was great in the earth, and that every imagination of the thoughts of his heart was only evil continually.

Your life is going in the direction of your dominant thoughts. You can't go anywhere in your physical body that you haven't already been in your mind. That's a huge statement.

Strong's definition for *yetser*[9] is "conception." I believe that your imagination is where you conceive things. Just as a woman has to conceive a child in her womb, you have to conceive your miracle in your imagination. A stork doesn't deliver babies, and a woman doesn't just go to the hospital and have a baby given to her. She has to conceive a baby and then give birth.

In a similar way, you conceive what God wants you to do in your imagination. Your imagination has the miraculous power to conceive things. It is your spiritual womb.

Being born again, not of corruptible seed, but of incorruptible, by the word of God, which liveth and abideth for ever.

1 Peter 1:23

The Greek word for seed there is *spora*,[10] which is a derivative of the Greek word *sperma*.[11] It's saying that the Word of God is like a seed—a sperm—and it has to be planted in your heart (imagination) to conceive.

For you to conceive a miracle, you have to use your imagination. If it's foolish for a woman to just pray for a child but never have a physical relationship with a man, it is just as foolish for you to pray for healing but never see yourself healed in your imagination.

Don't Think Small

Yea, they turned back and tempted God, and limited the Holy One of Israel.

Psalm 78:41

How you use your imagination determines whether you are a success or a failure. You have to focus on the right things and see God's best for you if you want those things to manifest in your life. If you focus on negative things, Satan will speak to you through them, you will magnify those things, and you will conceive failure in your heart.

I've known talented people who had the ability to be successful, but for whatever reason, they had an image on the inside of themselves of being a failure. Maybe you've felt that way. Whether it's someone who abused you or told you that you would never amount to anything, how you let those thoughts influence your imagination will create a self-fulfilling prophecy. Proverbs 23:7 says, *"For as [a man] thinketh in his heart, so is he."*

A good friend of mine once told me how his dad used junk cars for parts. They had junk cars parked on their farm, and his dad would take parts out of one to repair something else. Every time my friend helped repair the cars, his dad would say, "You're so stupid! You can't screw a nut on a bolt without cross-threading it."

After years of hearing that message, it became a self-fulfilling prophecy in my friend's life. I remember working on a car with him. As smart and capable as my friend was, he'd shake every time he had to put a nut on a bolt—terrified he'd cross-thread it. One time, my friend had put the nut on just fine, but he was so afraid he had cross-threaded it. So, he took the nut off and put it on again. He kept doing it until he eventually cross-threaded that bolt. To this day, I've never seen my friend put a nut on a bolt that wasn't cross-threaded. That's the way he saw himself.

The way you see yourself is the way you're going to be. Not long after God really touched my life in 1968, I knew I was going to have a ministry that influenced millions of people all over the world. Then, one of the most important days in the history of this ministry was January 31, 2002, when the Lord told me I had limited Him by my small thinking. Although I knew the vision God had for this ministry, I never allowed myself to see it on the inside of me. There were a lot of reasons for that, but the Lord finally got through to me with Psalm 78:41. So, I began to just let my imagination work and change the image on the inside of me.

Keep a Good Heart

O generation of vipers, how can ye, being evil, speak good things? for out of the abundance of the heart the mouth speaketh.

Matthew 12:34

The fourth key to staying full of God is maintaining a good heart. Your heart is a major topic in the Bible. It controls what you say and do. It's the essence of who you are. But most people don't understand this. They're more familiar with what's called "behavior modification." They are trying to change their actions without changing their heart.

It doesn't matter what you do—your heart attitude is more important than your actions. The Lord is more concerned about your heart because if your heart is right, your actions will be right. Religious people hate to hear this. They're more concerned with the form and outward action (external) than truly dealing with the heart (internal).

Years ago, we pastored a church in Childress, Texas, and one day we took a small group out to the park for a picnic. We came across a family—a husband, wife, and their two-year-old daughter—who had just left the nudist colony they were living in. They were totally broke, so they came over and begged us for some food.

We gave them something to eat and began sharing the Gospel with them. We led this couple to the Lord, they became born again, and they started coming to church. Since they'd been in a nudist colony, the woman only had short shorts and halter tops to wear, so that's what she came to church in. During praise and worship, she'd go to dancing and praising God, and it just left little to the imagination! It ended up causing some problems with other people in the church.

Several of them came to me, demanding, "Aren't you going to tell her that she needs to put some clothes on?" I answered, "She just became born again. Let her enjoy the fact that God loves her. He'll show her in time. But in the meantime, I'm not going to condemn her." We allowed this woman to keep coming to church and let God's love work in her heart.

One day, she came to one of Jamie's Bible studies, stood up, and told the ladies, "I have never owned a dress in all my life. I would really like to have one. Would you all pray with me?" They not only prayed with her, but within an hour after that Bible study, she had a dozen dresses that were all up to her neck and all the way down to the floor!

She came to church that night showing off her dress and praising God, saying, "Look at what the Lord did!" No one condemned her. It just worked out. God was more pleased with that woman coming to church in her short shorts and halter top than many Christians who have never dressed that way. Why? Because her heart was right. She was in love with Jesus and worshiping Him.

Actions Follow the Heart

This I say therefore, and testify in the Lord, that ye henceforth walk not as other Gentiles walk, in the vanity of their mind, having the understanding darkened, being alienated from the life of God through the ignorance that is in them, because of the blindness of their heart.

Ephesians 4:17–18

God wants to change your heart, and when I refer to your heart, I'm talking about the combination of your spirit and your soul—not your physical heart. To understand this concept of the heart completely, you must understand that you are a spirit, you have a soul (often referred to as your mind, will, and emotions), and you live in a body. So, once your heart is changed, your actions will change. Actions are not the driving force; they follow. Right actions are a by-product of an intimate relationship with God. I'm not telling you to act ungodly. I'm just saying that it needs to come from your heart, or it doesn't please God. It may please religious people, but God looks at your heart (1 Sam. 16:7).

It doesn't matter that you're doing the right things. You could give all you have to feed the poor, and even die a martyr's death, but if you're not motivated by God's kind of love, it'll profit you nothing (1 Cor. 13:3). If you're going to do anything, it has to come from a pure heart of love.

Mankind was originally created to be in fellowship with God. He spoke to us in our spirits because our hearts were in constant communion with Him. Our hearts dictated what we thought, felt, and did. When man sinned against God, that communion was broken, and their spirits died. They became separated from God.

When a person is born again, they become a brand-new creature. The old man passes away, and the spirit is made brand new (2 Cor. 5:17). You can let your heart lead you instead of your carnal mind and external circumstances (2 Cor. 5:7). But very few Christians are doing that. They are not renewing their minds to God's Word (Rom. 12:2).

Once, when I was ministering in Phoenix, I noticed a woman bouncing up and down on the front row. She was excited because she had just been born again two months before. I asked her to come up and share her testimony. But when she did, it seemed like every third word she used was profanity. People gasped, and some laughed.

She looked at me and asked, "Did I do something wrong?" I answered, "No, you didn't do anything wrong. Just keep going." So, she cussed up a storm for ten minutes, but she was excited for the Lord and experiencing His love for her.

Afterward, people came to me and criticized how she spoke. They were judging her outwardly and totally missing her heart. I said, "This woman loves God with all her heart. Her brain just hasn't caught up yet."

When I returned a year later, she came up to me and apologized, saying, "I'm sorry! I didn't know Christians don't talk like that." She had come out of being a prostitute and thought everyone used profanity. But over time, she'd gotten in the Word; and because her heart was right, it began to bear fruit. Her behavior changed as a by-product of her relationship with God.

Stay Sensitive to God

When the apostle Paul talked about someone being like a gentile in Ephesians 4:17, he was referring to someone who lived outside of God's covenant. Today, it would be like someone who doesn't know Jesus as Lord and Savior. Paul is saying, "Don't be like a lost person who just lives out of their brain and not their heart."

The issues of life flow out of your heart (Prov. 4:23). You need to learn to listen to your heart. But when your heart becomes hardened—cold, insensitive, unfeeling, and unyielding to God—it may still function, but it becomes sensitive toward physical, fleshly types of things.

Sad to say, this is where the vast majority of Christians live. Our hearts are conditioned to be sensitive to and dominated by our physical senses. If you really examine the fruit of your life and discover you are living no better than your unsaved neighbors, your heart may be hardened.

Your heart becomes sensitive to whatever you focus your attention on, and your heart becomes hardened to whatever you neglect. If you would glorify, magnify, and value God, then you would put a greater priority upon the Lord and His Word. He would occupy more of your focus and attention than other things. If you start being thankful, you'll humble yourself and direct your attention away from negative things and put it on positive things.

If you glorify and thank God, your imagination will start seeing godly things instead of the negative. The end result is that your heart will become sensitive to God. This isn't really hard to do—it's easy! But if you're neglecting the things of God and listening to the doubt, unbelief, fear, anger, criticism, and negativity of the world, there is no way your heart will be sensitive to Him. You can still retain knowledge, but it isn't dominating you anymore. You're insensitive because of the condition of your heart.

Don't Get Burned Out

Staying full of God is important for every believer—it's not something limited to "super saints"—but it's especially important for ministers. It's been said that four out of five ministers quit within the first five years.[12] Of the 20 percent who remain in ministry, a poll from 2021 reported that 38 percent of pastors were considering quitting.[13] These ministers are on the verge of burnout! And these are the people who are supposed to train up the body of Christ for the work of the ministry (Eph. 4:11–13)!

If you are serving God, you've got a big target drawn on you. When I was in the military in Vietnam, I served on a fire support base. I saw a colonel walking toward me one day, so I stopped and saluted. That colonel knocked me down, stood over me, and said, "If you ever see this bald head coming toward you again, you'd better turn and go the other way!"

You see, before I was deployed overseas, I got in trouble for not properly saluting my superiors. I don't know what it was about giving a salute, but I just had a hard time doing it. The situation got so serious that I was threatened with discipline—so, I started saluting everything that moved!

As I was lying there on the ground with that colonel standing over me, I thought, *Which is it? Do I salute or not salute?*

He explained to me that enemy snipers were watching that fire support base, and if they saw someone get saluted, they would know he was an officer. Officers were at higher risk of being shot because they were leaders. A leader was a more valuable target.

If God has destined for you to be in any position of influence and leadership, I guarantee you are going to be attacked. You're going to have people criticize you, and that can lead to burnout. Satan is going to try and drain you of the fullness of God and get your focus off Him.

A person who is burned out is really just someone who's doing things in their own strength and ability. They've stopped glorifying God and have shifted their focus to the attacks. They've forgotten about all the good things God has already done for them. They begin to imagine what it looks like to be defeated. Finally, they lose heart. When that happens, they are fighting from a position of defeat rather than victory. They're no longer living from God's fullness.

The Vacuum Within

I remember a science experiment my sixth-grade teacher did. He put a small one-gallon metal gas can on a Bunsen burner and heated it. Then as soon as it got hot, he put the cap back on really tight. He set that can on his desk and just kept on teaching. As the air cooled, it formed a partial vacuum on the inside of that can. Since I was sitting there in the front row, I can vividly remember watching that can.

It started crackling and popping without anyone touching it. Then—all of a sudden—it became crushed. It looked to me like someone had taken a sledgehammer to it. That can just fell to the floor and continued getting crushed. I watched the entire scenario. Nobody touched it. This was just natural atmospheric pressure acting on a can with nothing inside.

It's the vacuum within—not the pressure without— that's causing people to be crushed today. Under normal circumstances, the pressure within would not have crushed the can. However, the absence of pressure within caused normal atmospheric pressure to crush it.

Some people just can't handle the pressure on their lives because they aren't thinking about what is already inside them. They spend their time talking about how bad things are, putting great value on the pressure to sin, or just give up on God. It just makes them feel justified in their failures and how they feel.

I once had someone in our Bible school come to me with a complaint, and this person always seemed to have something to complain about! This time, they were crying about how they were in a service, trying to listen to the message, but two ladies sat in front of them and talked the whole time. So, this person was upset that Satan stole the Word from them. My only question was, "Why didn't you get up and move?"

A negative attitude kept this person from staying full of God. They didn't magnify God, but instead, they focused their attention on something relatively trivial and let it ruin their experience.

In contrast, I had just gotten off the phone with a friend whose wife had passed away. I was calling to check on him, but instead of crying about how bad things were, he was just rejoicing in the Lord. He was thanking God for all the years they had together and rejoicing that she was with Jesus. Now that's a godly attitude! By remembering the good things of God and thanking Him for a lifetime of marriage, this man was staying full. He wasn't letting circumstances negatively influence him.

Consider what Jesus suffered for you (Heb. 12:2–4). Until you've suffered to the point that it costs you your life, you have no right to complain. If you're alive, you ought to be praising God!

Stop the Ups and Downs

Every valley shall be exalted, and every mountain and hill shall be made low: and the crooked shall be made straight, and the rough places plain.

Isaiah 40:4

The Bible says that a day would come when the valleys would be raised up, and the mountains and hills would be brought low. If you bring the valleys up and the mountains down, that should make for smooth sailing. I'm not saying that we live without problems. I have all kinds of problems and have had terrible things happen to me, but those things have never diminished the love of God and the revelation of what He's done in my life. It's only grown and gotten stronger.

The vast majority of the body of Christ embraces their up-and-down experience and thinks that it's God—that it's just the way He does things. They've even come up with these sermons where God will take you off of the mountaintop and lead you down into the valley because that's where the water is, and fruit grows in the valley. So, you have to go through these high-and-low experiences for your own good. But Jesus said if you come to Him, you'll never hunger or thirst again (John 6:35–38).

Someone may be thinking, *Well, should we live as Christians based on what Jesus said or by what people experience?* It's actually both. In your born-again spirit, you have received the fullness of God, including love, joy, peace, longsuffering, gentleness, goodness, faith, meekness, and temperance (Gal. 5:22–23). You have been made a brand-new creature in your spirit (2 Cor. 5:17)! But you aren't just a spirit.

You're also a soul in a body. And the sad fact is many people are focused on the physical, natural things of their lives instead of who they are in Christ. They are living in the flesh instead of in the spirit. And because of it, people aren't experiencing this constant flow of love, joy, and peace. But that's not God's fault! The Lord put all of His goodness inside us, but we have to work it out (Phil. 2:12–13).

It is necessary that you know who you are in your born-again spirit. You are the righteousness of God in

Christ (2 Cor. 5:21)! Before you see the goodness of God manifest in your life, you have to renew your mind by sowing God's Word in your heart. We won't benefit from the truths found in God's Word until we convince ourselves of them.

Be Satisfied

Jesus answered and said unto her, Whosoever drinketh of this water shall thirst again: but whosoever drinketh of the water that I shall give him shall never thirst; but the water that I shall give him shall be in him a well of water springing up into everlasting life.

John 4:13–14

Jesus was speaking to the woman at the well, but He wasn't talking about just physical water. He said that once you receive Him, you will no longer spiritually thirst. You will be satisfied in your spirit.

Jesus was using the example of drinking water to describe how the Lord satisfies our spiritual thirst with the living water of the Holy Spirit. In other words, if you receive salvation, you will never thirst (spiritually) again.

In John 6, we learn that a group sought after Jesus, but for the wrong reasons. Jesus had already performed a great miracle before them in feeding the 5,000 (vv. 1–14), but the people's hearts were so set on themselves that they missed the true miracle. At first, they tried to take Jesus by force and make Him king, but He escaped, and they followed Him to Capernaum (vv. 15–25). When the people confronted Him,

> *Jesus answered them and said, Verily, verily, I say unto you, Ye seek me, not because ye saw the miracles, but because ye did eat of the loaves, and were filled.*

John 6:26

They only perceived how good it felt to have their physical hunger satisfied. Jesus revealed that the motives behind people's actions are more important than the actions themselves. The priority should be on spiritual things and not physical things. Although seeing bread materialize would have been a great miracle, it would have been insignificant compared to the miracle of God being manifested in the flesh (1 Tim. 3:16). They were obviously blind to that fact that they were talking to the very Son of Man—the greatest miracle that God had ever performed.

And Jesus said unto them, I am the bread of life: he that cometh to me shall never hunger; and he that believeth on me shall never thirst.

John 6:35

Despite what Jesus taught, many Christians say, "I'm so hungry, and I'm so thirsty for the Lord!" They even write songs about it and sing about how desperate they are for God. It just goes to show that some people just won't let the Bible get in the way of what they believe.

I understand the point that they're trying to get across—that we're supposed to be seeking the Lord. But it's wrong for a Christian to claim they are hungry and thirsty when the Lord has said, *"he that cometh to me shall never hunger; and ... never thirst."* If you've received Jesus as Lord, you have the fullness of God in you already (Col. 2:6–10)!

It's comparable to sitting at a table with a feast set before you. You may be hungry, but it's not because you don't have access to food. If you're hungry, just eat. Stop talking about being hungry and partake of what's in front of you. Likewise, the Lord has prepared everything you could ever need and placed it inside of you. Quit singing about how hungry you are and start partaking of what's already been provided by glorifying the Lord, being thankful for what He has done, using your imagination to see victory instead of defeat, and set your heart on the good things of the Lord.

Conclusion

The process revealed in Romans 1:21 can either lead you away from God, or it can bring you back to Him. Now, I'm not condemning anyone, but I believe we are living well below where God actually wants us to be. The Bible says it's the goodness of God that brings people to repentance (Rom. 2:4). I believe that if you follow the keys detailed in this booklet, you'll turn your life around and begin experiencing that goodness to a greater degree—and it won't run out!

Make a conscious decision to glorify God. Place more value on the Lord, what He's said, and what He's done in your life than anything or anyone else. Don't seek the acclaim of people. You have to get to the place where your love for and commitment to God stands alone. Even if everything else in your life fell apart, decide that you would still esteem, honor, and put more importance on Him—and His Word!

When I was in the military in Vietnam, I began to sow the Word of God into my heart and put down deep roots.

Because of that, I've continued glorifying God and placing value on who He is and what He's done. I've let the Word act like a seed and conceive miracles in my imagination. And, through it all, I've kept my heart right and drawn on the close intimate relationship I have with the Lord.

These things have grown and sustained my life and ministry. But God is not a respecter of persons (Rom. 2:11). I believe you can put these same truths to work in your own life and see the same results! Praise the Lord!

Magnify the Lord and make Him bigger. Praise Him, thank Him, and rehearse your victories. Make a conscious effort to minimize the negative, set joy before you, and fix your eyes on the good things God has done. If you'll do this, your imagination will start seeing positive things, and your heart will become sensitized to God.

If you receive these four keys to staying full of God and start implementing them in your daily life, you'll experience a radical transformation. This could change your life forever, but it all depends on what you do with it. What value will you place on what you've learned? Only you can decide.

FURTHER STUDY

If you enjoyed this booklet and would like to learn more about some of the things I've shared, I suggest my teachings:

- *Discover the Keys to Staying Full of God (complete teaching)*
- *Don't Limit God*
- *The Positive Ministry of the Holy Spirit*
- *The Word Became Flesh*
- *Effortless Change*
- *Hardness of Heart*

These teachings are available for free at **awmi.net**, or they can be purchased at **awmi.net/store**.

Go deeper in your relationship with God by browsing all of Andrew's free teachings.

Receive Jesus as Your Savior

Choosing to receive Jesus Christ as your Lord and Savior is the most important decision you'll ever make!

God's Word promises, *"That if thou shalt confess with thy mouth the Lord Jesus, and shalt believe in thine heart that God hath raised him from the dead, thou shalt be saved. For with the heart man believeth unto righteousness; and with the mouth confession is made unto salvation"* (Rom. 10:9–10). *"For whosoever shall call upon the name of the Lord shall be saved"* (Rom. 10:13). By His grace, God has already done everything to provide salvation. Your part is simply to believe and receive.

Pray out loud: "Jesus, I acknowledge that I've sinned and need to receive what you did for the forgiveness of my sins. I confess that You are my Lord and Savior. I believe in my heart that God raised You from the dead. By faith in Your Word, I receive salvation now. Thank You for saving me."

The very moment you commit your life to Jesus Christ, the truth of His Word instantly comes to pass in your spirit. Now that you're born again, there's a brand-new you!

Please contact us and let us know that you've prayed to receive Jesus as your Savior. We'd like to send you some free materials to help you on your new journey. Call our Helpline: **719-635-1111** (available 24 hours a day, seven days a week) to speak to a staff member who is here to help you understand and grow in your new relationship with the Lord.

Welcome to your new life!

Receive the Holy Spirit

As His child, your loving heavenly Father wants to give you the supernatural power you need to live a new life. *"For every one that asketh receiveth; and he that seeketh findeth; and to him that knocketh it shall be opened…how much more shall* your *heavenly Father give the Holy Spirit to them that ask him?"* (Luke 11:10–13).

All you have to do is ask, believe, and receive! Pray this: "Father, I recognize my need for Your power to live a new life. Please fill me with Your Holy Spirit. By faith, I receive it right now. Thank You for baptizing me. Holy Spirit, You are welcome in my life."

Some syllables from a language you don't recognize will rise up from your heart to your mouth (1 Cor. 14:14). As you speak them out loud by faith, you're releasing God's power from within and building yourself up in the spirit (1 Cor. 14:4). You can do this whenever and wherever you like.

It doesn't really matter whether you felt anything or not when you prayed to receive the Lord and His Spirit. If you believed in your heart that you received, then God's Word promises you did. *"Therefore I say unto you, What things soever ye desire, when ye pray, believe that ye receive* them, *and ye shall have* them" (Mark 11:24). God always honors His Word—believe it!

We would like to rejoice with you, pray with you, and answer any questions to help you understand more fully what has taken place in your life!

Please contact us to let us know that you've prayed to be filled with the Holy Spirit and to request the book *The New You & the Holy Spirit.* This book will explain in more detail about the benefits of being filled with the Holy Spirit and speaking in tongues. Call our Helpline: **719-635-1111** (available 24 hours a day, seven days a week).

Endnotes

1. The American Heritage Dictionary of the English Language, s.v. "reprobate," accessed August 23, 2023, https://ahdictionary.com/word/search.html?q=reprobate.

2. Strong's Definitions, s.v. "δοξάζω" ("doxazō"), accessed August 23, 2023, https://www.blueletterbible.org/lexicon/g1392/kjv/tr/0-1/.

3. Merriam-Webster Dictionary, s.v. "esteem," accessed August 23, 2023, https://www.merriam-webster.com/dictionary/esteem.

4. Blue Letter Bible, s.v. "δοξάζω" ("doxazō"), accessed August 28, 2023, https://www.blueletterbible.org/lexicon/g1392/kjv/tr/0-1/.

5. Strong's Definitions, s.v. "μεριμνάω" ("merimnaō"), accessed September 5, 2023, https://www.blueletterbible.org/lexicon/g3309/kjv/tr/0-1/.

6. James Sturcke, "Bird flu pandemic 'could kill 150m,'" The Guardian, September 30, 2005, https://www.theguardian.com/world/2005/sep/30/birdflu.jamessturcke.

7. "Cumulative number of confirmed human cases for avian influenza A(H5N1) reported to WHO, 2003–2023," World Health Organization, accessed September 5, 2023, https://cdn.who.int/media/docs/default-source/influenza/human-animal-interface-risk-assessments/cumulative-

number-of-confirmed-human-cases-for-avian-influenza-a(h5n1)-reported-to-who--2003-2023d4e36995-440c-423a-98f6-0d2a763c8438.pdf?sfvrsn=c58756a1.

8. Charles Capps, "Decrees: Their Force & Power," Harrison House, Accessed August 30, 2023, https://harrisonhouse.com/blog/charles-capps-decrees-their-force-and-power.

9. Strong's Definitions, s.v. "יֵצֶר" ("yēṣer"), accessed August 30, 2023, https://www.blueletterbible.org/lexicon/h3336/kjv/wlc/0-1/.

10. Blue Letter Bible, s.v. "σπορά" ("spora"), accessed August 30, 2023, https://www.blueletterbible.org/lexicon/g4701/kjv/tr/0-1/.

11. Blue Letter Bible, s.v. "σπέρμα" ("sperma"), accessed August 30, 2023, https://www.blueletterbible.org/lexicon/g4690/kjv/tr/0-1/.

12. Trisha R. Peach, "Burnout, Timeout, and Fallout: A Qualitative Study of Why Pastors Leave Ministry," (Doctoral thesis, Bethel University, 2022), 7, 49-50, and 134, https://spark.bethel.edu/cgi/viewcontent.cgi?article=1804&context=etd.

13. Kate Shellnutt, "The Pastors Aren't All Right: 38% Consider Leaving Ministry," Christianity Today. November 16, 2021, https://www.christianitytoday.com/news/2021/november/pastor-burnout-pandemic-barna-consider-leaving-ministry.html.

Call for Prayer

If you need prayer for any reason, you can call our Helpline, 24 hours a day, seven days a week at **719-635-1111**. A trained prayer minister will answer your call and pray with you.

Every day, we receive testimonies of healings and other miracles from our Helpline, and we are ministering God's nearly-too-good-to-be-true message of the Gospel to more people than ever. So, I encourage you to call today!

About the Author

Andrew Wommack's life was forever changed the moment he encountered the supernatural love of God on March 23, 1968. As a renowned Bible teacher and author, Andrew has made it his mission to change the way the world sees God.

Andrew's vision is to go as far and deep with the Gospel as possible. His message goes far through the *Gospel Truth* television program, which is available to over half the world's population. The message goes deep through discipleship at Charis Bible College, headquartered in Woodland Park, Colorado. Founded in 1994, Charis has campuses across the United States and around the globe.

Andrew also has an extensive library of teaching materials in print, audio, and video. More than 200,000 hours of free teachings can be accessed at **awmi.net**.

Contact Information

Andrew Wommack Ministries, Inc.

PO Box 3333
Colorado Springs, CO 80934-3333
info@awmi.net
awmi.net

Helpline: 719-635-1111 (available 24/7)

Charis Bible College

info@charisbiblecollege.org
844-360-9577
CharisBibleCollege.org

For a complete list of all of our offices,
visit **awmi.net/contact-us**.

Connect with us on social media.

Andrew's
LIVING COMMENTARY
BIBLE SOFTWARE

Andrew Wommack's *Living Commentary* Bible study software is a user-friendly, downloadable program. It's like reading the Bible with Andrew at your side, sharing his revelation with you verse by verse.

Main features:
- Bible study software with a grace-and-faith perspective
- Over 26,000 notes by Andrew on verses from Genesis through Revelation
- *Matthew Henry's Concise Commentary*
- 12 Bible versions
- 2 concordances: *Englishman's Concordance* and *Strong's Concordance*
- 2 dictionaries: *Collaborative International Dictionary* and *Holman's Dictionary*
- Atlas with biblical maps
- Bible and *Living Commentary* statistics
- Quick navigation, including history of verses
- Robust search capabilities (for the Bible and Andrew's notes)
- "Living" (i.e., constantly updated and expanding)
- Ability to create personal notes

Whether you're new to studying the Bible or a seasoned Bible scholar, you'll gain a deeper revelation of the Word from a grace-and-faith perspective.

Purchase Andrew's *Living Commentary* today at **awmi.net/living**, and grow in the Word with Andrew.

Item code: 8350

ANDREW WOMMACK MINISTRIES